D0946575

If The Sky Could Talk...

Written by Stuart A. Kallen

Illustrated by Kristen Copham

Published by Abdo & Daughters, 4940 Viking Drive Suite 622, Edina, Minnesota 55435.

Library bound edition distributed by Rockbottom Books, Pentagon Towers, P.O. Box 36036, Minneapolis, Minnesota 55435.

Edited by Julie Berg

Kallen, Stuart A., 1955 -
    If the Sky could Talk / written by Stuart A. Kallen.
        p. cm. -- (Target Earth)
    Summary: Discusses the importance of the layers of the earth's atmosphere and the need to prevent air pollution.
    ISBN 1-56239-185-2
    1. Atmosphere--Juvenile literature. [1. Atmosphere. 2. Air-pollution. 3. Pollution.] I. Title. II. Series.
    QC863.5.K35   1993
    551.5--dc20   93-10177
                                                       CIP
                                                       AC

Thanks To The Trees From Which This Recycled Paper Was First Made.

Abdo & Daughters
Minneapolis

This is what it would say...

Float through the air with the greatest of ease!

Travel to the outer limits of space.

Learn what's in the sky—let the clouds be your guide.

HELLO DOWN THERE!!! It's me, the sky. I've come out of the clear blue to talk to you.

I, the sky, am above it all. Birds fly in me. Space shuttles streak through me. Clouds float inside of me. Lightning crackles around me, and rainbows arch across me.

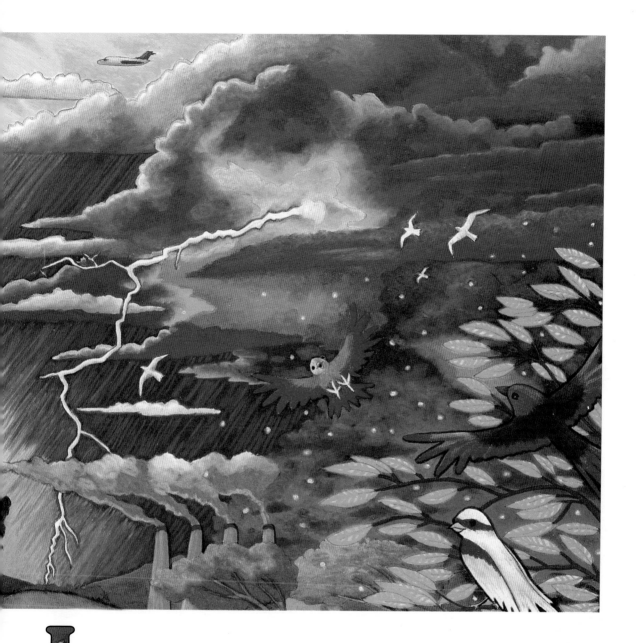

I, the sky, hold the air you breathe. I protect you from the sun's burning rays. I carry away smoke from cars and factories. I whip up the winds. I help make rain, snow, and storms.

At night, you can look up to me and see the distant stars twinkling.

My real name is the *atmosphere*. That's a big word, but if you say it like three words, you can learn to say it right. At. Mo. Sphere. Atmosphere!

I wrap myself around the Earth and protect all life on the planet.

Big, white, puffy clouds float in me. Clouds are formed when the sun heats up the ground. This makes the warm air rise. That air cools as it rises higher and higher. As the air cools, tiny water droplets are released. The droplets gather together to form clouds.

Sometimes when it rains you see rainbows—those beautiful bands of red, orange, yellow, green, blue, and purple. Rainbows appear when sunlight shines through rain.

When the clouds become heavy with too much water, they let go of it. That's what we call rain! If the water freezes, it will fall as snow, ice, or sleet. Neat!

I, the sky, have several layers. Each one of the layers does a different job. The lowest layer of the atmosphere is called the *troposphere*. Say it like three words. Tro. Po. Sphere. Troposphere! This is the layer where the weather is made. If you've ever flown in a jet airplane, you have flown at the top of the troposphere, which is six miles (10 kilometers) high.

The next layer up is the *stratosphere*. Say it like three words. Strat. O. Sphere. Stratosphere! In the stratosphere, the air is very thin and very, very cold. My ozone layer is in the stratosphere. It protects all life on Earth from the sun's harmful rays.

One problem facing the Earth is a growing hole in the ozone layer. The hole in the ozone is caused by pollution. Scientists are trying to figure out ways to stop the hole from growing. Then the Earth will not be damaged.

The biggest threat to the sky is pollution. Millions of cars, trucks, and buses use gasoline every day. All that burned gas makes smoke called *air pollution*. Sometimes the smoke makes plants, animals, and humans sick.

My stratosphere layer is six to thirty-one miles (10 to 50 kilometers) high. That's a mighty high sky!

My next layer is called the *ionosphere*. Say it like four words. I. On. O. Sphere. Ionosphere! The ionosphere is where spaceships and satellites orbit the Earth. Space shuttles fly through the ionosphere. The ionosphere is 40 to 450 miles (67 to 760 kilometers) high.

People need to drive less and make cars that run

cleaner. Then air pollution won't make me brown and dirty.

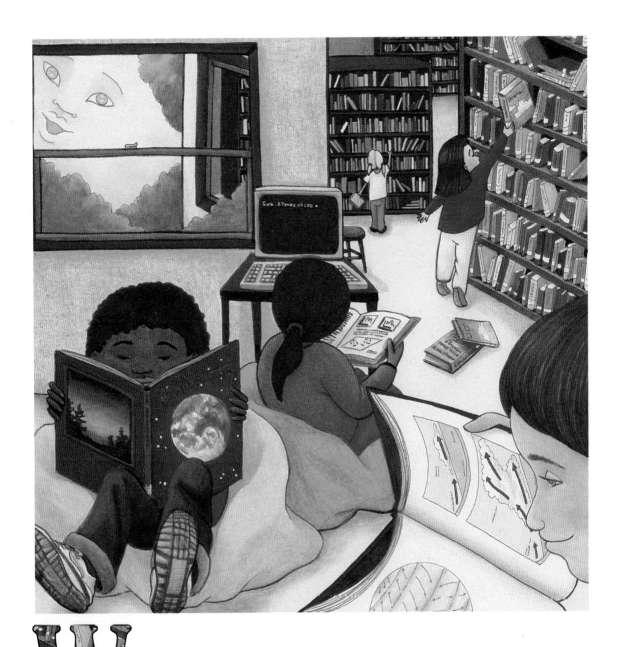

Well those were big words to describe the clear blue sky. There are even more layers and names for me. You can read about them in library books.

So remember, when you lay on your back with your eye to the sky, there is more to the sky than meets the eye.

Goodbye!

Glossary

Atmosphere — The air surrounding the Earth.

Clouds — A white or gray mass in the sky, made up of tiny drops of water.

Ionosphere — Part of the Earth's atmosphere beginning at an altitude of 30 miles (50 kilometers) and extending outward 300 miles (500 kilometers).

Lightning — A flash of electricity in the sky.

Ozone layer — The upper layer of the Earth's atmosphere containing ozone gas that blocks out the sun's harmful rays.

Pollution — Harming the environment by putting man-made wastes in the air, water and ground.

Rainbows — An arch of colored light seen in the sky opposite the sun.

Satellite — A man-made object that orbits the Earth.

Stratosphere — An upper portion of the Earth's atmosphere that is 7 miles (11 kilometers) high.

Troposphere — A portion of the Earth's atmosphere which is below the stratosphere.

Eco–Activities

1 Watch a show on-public television (PBS) about air pollution and the ozone layer. Look at a listing of television shows, like the *TV Guide*, and find a show you think you might like. Pay close attention to the parts of the show that talk about air pollution and the ozone layer.

2 Make a paper airplane. Fly it indoors. Fly it outdoors. Notice how the wind changes the flight of the plane. Change the shape of the plane to make it fly better. If you don't know how to make a paper airplane, ask someone to show you how.

3 Go fly a kite! Notice how the wind controls the kite.

4 If you live in the city, this experiment will show you how much pollution is in the air. Take a piece of white paper and lay it on the ground outdoors. Weigh the paper down with small rocks on each corner. Leave the paper on the ground for several days when the weather is dry. Compare the paper to a clean sheet of paper. The dirt and dust on the paper is from air pollution.

E~co~ – F~acts~

MORE FOAM FACTS: Styrofoam will not break down. The cup you used for breakfast will be here five-hundred years from now. Every year, Americans produce enough styrofoam cups to circle the Earth 436 times!

FOAM ALONE: Styrofoam cups, plates, and coolers release gases that destroy the ozone layer when they break apart. Don't use styrofoam. If your school cafeteria uses styrofoam, ask them to switch to paper.

FEET, GET MOVING: Cars are the biggest cause of air pollution. Walk, ride your bike, or use the bus. Ask your family to drive less and walk more. It's more fun, healthier, and better for the planet.

Write or Call

Natural Resources Defense Council
40 West 20th Street
New York, NY 10011
Ask for pamphlet, "Saving the Ozone Layer"
212-727-2700

The Global Releaf Program
P.O. Box 2000
Washington, D.C., 20013
Ask for information,
202-667-3300

Kids Against Pollution
P.O. Box 775
Closter, N.J., 07624
Ask for information,
201-784-0668

TARGET EARTH™ COMMITMENT

At Target, we're committed to the environment. We show this commitment not only through our own internal efforts but also through the programs we sponsor in the communities where we do business.

Our commitment to children and the environment began when we became the Founding International Sponsor for Kids for Saving Earth, a non-profit environmental organization for kids. We helped launch the program in 1989 and supported its growth to three-quarters of a million club members in just three years.

Our commitment to children's environmental education led to the development of an environmental curriculum called Target Earth™, aimed at getting kids involved in their education and in their world.

In addition, we worked with Abdo & Daughters Publishing to develop the Target Earth™ Earthmobile, an environmental science library on wheels that can be used in libraries, or rolled from classroom to classroom.

Target believes that the children are our future and the future of our planet. Through education, they will save the world!

Minneapolis-based Target Stores is an upscale discount department store chain of 517 stores in 33 states coast-to-coast, and is the largest division of Dayton Hudson Corporation, one of the nation's leading retailers.